Sally Ride
Science

SALLY RIDE & TAM O'SHAUGHNESSY

MISSION PLANET EARTH

OUR WORLD AND ITS CLIMATE—AND HOW HUMANS ARE CHANGING THEM

ROARING BROOK PRESS
NEW YORK

To the scientists who figure out how and why Earth's
climate is changing;
to the science writers who let the world know what
the scientists learn;
and to the next generation of scientists who will find ways
to restore our planet's natural balance.

An innovative science education company.

Copyright © 2009 by Sally Ride and Tam O'Shaughnessy
Published by Flash Point, an imprint of Roaring Brook Press
Roaring Brook Press is a division of Holtzbrinck Publishing Holdings
Limited Partnership
175 Fifth Avenue, New York, New York 10010
All rights reserved

Distributed in Canada by H. B. Fenn and Company Ltd.

Cataloging-in-Publication Data is on file at the Library of Congress
ISBN-10: 1-59643-310-8
ISBN-13: 978-1-59643-310-6

Roaring Brook Press books are available for special promotions and premiums.
For details contact: Director of Special Markets, Holtzbrinck Publishers.

Illustrations and graphs created for this book by Jan Adkins. Copyright © 2009 by Jan Adkins.
Credits and permission to reprint photographs appear on page 79.

 This book is printed on paper containing a minimum 10% post-consumer waste.

First Edition March 2009
Printed in the United States of America
10 9 8 7 6 5 4 3 2 1

CONTENTS

MISSION: PLANET EARTH

When I was an astronaut, I spent hours gazing down at the Earth below. Our planet is beautiful. It's home to everything we know and hold dear.

When I looked out the window, I could see winding rivers emptying into blue oceans, mountainsides of a tropical rain forest, and muddy waters of river deltas. I could see city lights twinkle at night and contrails of airplanes criss-cross the sky.

More than anything, though, I could see how fragile Earth is. When I looked toward the horizon, I could see a thin, fuzzy blue line outlining the planet. At first, I didn't know what I was seeing. Then I realized it was Earth's atmosphere. It looked so thin and so fragile, like a strong gust of interplanetary wind could blow it all away. And I realized that this air is our planet's spacesuit—it's all that separates every bird, fish, and person on Earth from the blackness of space.

In the last few decades we've started to change that atmosphere. Some of the changes, like the smog hovering over Los Angeles, are even visible to astronauts in space. Others are invisible to the eye but are now easy to measure. The most dangerous—the one that will affect everything on our planet—is the warming that we now know we humans are causing.

Our warming climate is not visible to astronauts, but its effects will be. The next generation of astronauts could look down and see deserts where we now have lakes, meadows where we now have glaciers, and oceans where we now have beaches. Future astronauts may even have to launch into space from a new launch pad—Cape Canaveral could be underwater. They may look down and say, "That's where Washington, D.C., used to be," or "Did you know farmers used to grow wheat in Kansas?"

To a person standing on the ground, our air seems to go on forever. The sky looks so big, and people haven't worried about what they put into the air. From space, though, it's obvious how little air there really is. Nothing vanishes "into thin air." The gases that we're sending into the air are piling up in our atmosphere. And that's changing Earth's life-support system in ways that could change our planet forever.

The view from space, and the view from Earth: Photographed at sunrise from the window of the Space Shuttle, Earth's atmosphere is a thin, fragile blue band. Huge thunderstorms rise into the orange sky (previous page). From the prairies of Wyoming, the sky seems to stretch up endlessly (right).

EARTH:
IT'S ALL CONNECTED

Earth is getting warmer. And that's changing its climate.

What is "climate"? A lot of people think that climate and weather are the same thing. Yes, they are related to each other. But they're not the same. "Weather" is what you see when you step outside. You might see bright sunny skies and scattered clouds one day, then black clouds and heavy rain the next. Weather describes the conditions, such as temperature, clouds, rain, and wind, on a particular day and in a particular place.

Climates and ecosystems: the lush, temperate forests of the Blue Ridge Mountains in North Carolina (previous page); the hot, dry Sonoran Desert of the southwestern United States (above); and the vibrant coral reefs of the American Samoan islands in the Pacific Ocean (right).

Climate is the sum total of weather. It's determined over many years, and describes what the weather is usually like and what extremes to expect. If you live in Phoenix, you live in a hot, dry climate. That doesn't mean it never rains. But it does mean that there is less rain in a year than in most other places. If you live in Seattle, you live in a cool, damp climate. That doesn't mean you'll never go sunbathing, but on average it will be cooler and damper than, say, in Phoenix. You can talk about the climate of whatever size area you want. You can talk about the climate of the whole planet, or the climate of a country, a city, or even the climate of a particular meadow or mountainside.

Climates all around the world are changing. Why do we care about this? We, and all the other living things on the planet, have adapted to—and built lives around—the climates in our parts of the world. Polar bears in the Arctic, rattlesnakes in the desert, corals in the tropics, pine trees on cool mountaintops, and wheat farmers in Kansas all live where they do because the conditions in those places suit them. Now it's getting warmer everywhere. Snow and ice are melting, the oceans are getting warmer, and the deserts are getting drier. Spring is coming earlier, winter's not as cold, and the temperature doesn't fall as much

at night. Environments everywhere are changing. And the plants, animals, and people who live in those environments have to adapt or move.

Earth is a little like your body. Both have systems that work together to keep them healthy. Take a deep breath. Your respiratory system takes in oxygen and gets rid of carbon dioxide. Earth's respiratory system? Plants take in carbon dioxide from the air and release oxygen, while other living things—like people—breathe in oxygen and breathe out carbon dioxide.

Feel your heart beat. Your circulatory system moves your blood around, carrying oxygen to billions of cells in your body. Winds and ocean currents make up Earth's circulatory system. They carry heat and chemicals around our planet.

From the time our planet's land, oceans, and atmosphere formed, they have been connected to each other. The motion of air and water moves heat around the planet. The water cycle carries moisture from the oceans, through the air, to the land, and back to the oceans. Other cycles transport nutrients around the planet. Once life evolved, plants and animals became a part of these cycles, too. Today, these cycles maintain our planet's livable conditions. They moderate extreme temperatures and keep the composition of the air and oceans about the same from year to year. They move chemical elements like carbon, nitrogen, and oxygen back and forth between the environment and the living things that depend on them.

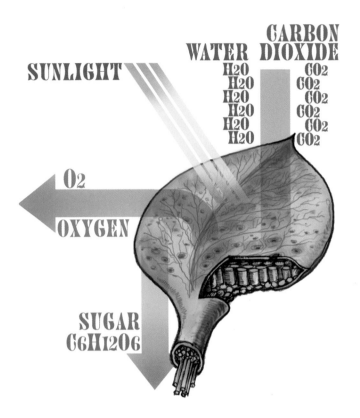

SUNLIGHT

WATER
H2O
H2O
H2O
H2O
H2O
H2O

CARBON
DIOXIDE
CO2
CO2
CO2
CO2
CO2
CO2

O2

OXYGEN

SUGAR
C6H12O6

Photosynthesis: Billions upon billions of times every day, photosynthesis takes place in the cells of green plants on land and phytoplankton in water. The organisms use the energy in sunlight to reassemble molecules of water and carbon dioxide into sugars—the basis of virtually all life on Earth.

IN THE BEGINNING

Today, Earth is an oasis. Breathable air hugs our planet, deep oceans wrap most of its surface, and seven continents cover the rest. And life is everywhere! But it wasn't always that way.

4.6 billion years ago, Earth was a giant ball of molten rock. It had no oceans and no atmosphere. Red-hot lava erupted from volcanoes and cracks in the crust. Eventually, the surface cooled. But Earth's insides were still boiling hot. Steam and other gases escaped from the molten interior, and our early atmosphere was formed. That air was thick and made mostly of nitrogen, carbon dioxide, and water vapor—nothing like the oxygen-packed air we breathe today. As the atmosphere cooled, water vapor condensed to form dark clouds. Then torrential rain flooded the low basins and formed Earth's first oceans.

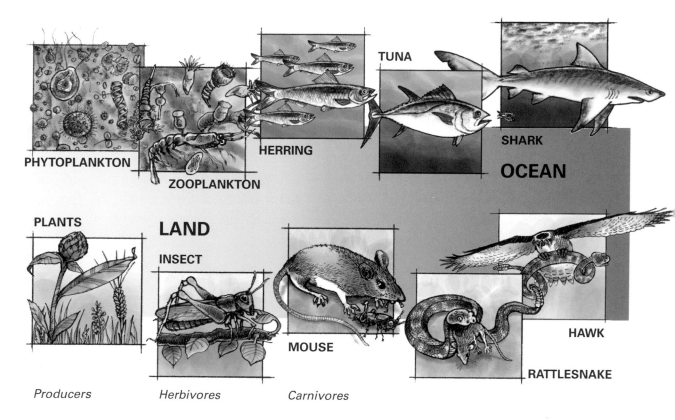

PHYTOPLANKTON ZOOPLANKTON HERRING TUNA SHARK OCEAN

PLANTS LAND INSECT MOUSE RATTLESNAKE HAWK

Producers   *Herbivores*   *Carnivores*

Two food chains: one land, one ocean. Producers (plants and phytoplankton) are consumed by plant-eating animals (herbivores), which are in turn consumed by other animals (carnivores)—all the way to the large predators at the "top" of food chains.

At first, there was no life on our planet. But primitive microscopic organisms evolved in the oceans. They were tiny, single cells that looked like today's bacteria. They stayed alive by taking in simple molecules from the water and using the energy released in chemical reactions. The tiny microbes divided again and again, and their numbers multiplied. Eventually, their microscopic descendants evolved the ability to make their own food through a process called photosynthesis. More than the wheel, the light bulb, the Internet, or any other human invention, this development changed the world.

Photosynthesis is the process by which some living things use the energy in sunlight to combine carbon dioxide and water molecules into sugar for food. As part of this process, oxygen is released. One by one, oxygen molecules began bubbling out of the ancient oceans and collecting in the air. Over the next two billion years, Earth's once unbreathable atmosphere slowly filled with oxygen.

Those tiny microbes were alone on the planet for two billion years. But they were about to have lots of company. All sorts of new life evolved—living things that breathed oxygen. And to this day, life on Earth depends on photosynthesis. The sugar molecules created by photosynthesis start almost all Earth's food chains, and the oxygen molecules released by photosynthesis are what we need when we breathe.

Today, phytoplankton in the ocean and their plant relatives on land carry out most photosynthesis—just like their ancient ancestors. It doesn't matter if you're a microbe or a mongoose, a clam or a college student—all living things need energy. But only plants and some microbes can turn the Sun's energy into an energy source the rest of us can use—food! All the rest of us depend on them for our survival.

THE GREENHOUSE

The sun powers our planet. It provides the light and heat that we and other living things depend on. Earth would be a frozen, lifeless rock without it. But the Sun is not the only thing that determines our climate. The amount of sunlight we receive is important—but so are the interactions of the oceans, atmosphere, land, and life. They determine how much of the Sun's heat is absorbed, and distribute it around the planet.

The Sun is constantly emitting energy in all directions. A tiny fraction of it falls on Earth. Some of the sunlight that does hit Earth is reflected right back out to space and doesn't warm our planet at all. It's reflected by clouds in the atmosphere and by ice and snow on the ground. But some sunlight is absorbed by our vast oceans and rocky land. That's the sunlight that warms the planet.

The warm ground cools off by radiating the heat back toward space. If this heat could make it back out through the atmosphere as easily as the sunlight makes it in, our planet would be much colder than it is.

But the heat doesn't escape so easily. Certain gases in the atmosphere absorb it before it makes it to space. Those gases re-radiate that heat in all directions. Some of it heads out toward space, but some heads back toward Earth. So some of the heat is trapped. This is called the greenhouse effect. Like the glass walls of a greenhouse, which let sunlight in but don't let all the heat out, the greenhouse effect in our atmosphere makes our planet warmer than it otherwise would be. It's almost like there is a thin blanket covering Earth.

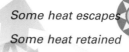

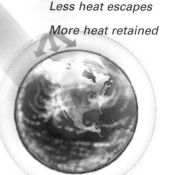

Some heat escapes

Some heat retained

Less heat escapes

More heat retained

Natural greenhouse
effect

Human-magnified
greenhouse effect

The greenhouse effect: The glass walls of a greenhouse let sunlight in, but don't let all the heat out (left). Greenhouse gases in the atmosphere do a similar thing, trapping some of the Sun's heat (center). The more greenhouse gases there are in the atmosphere, the more heat is trapped and the less escapes back into space (right).

The gases in the air that absorb heat in this way are called greenhouse gases. Not all the gases in the atmosphere are greenhouses gases; in fact, most of our air is made of gases that are not greenhouse gases. Oxygen and nitrogen make up approximately 99 percent of our atmosphere. If they made up 100 percent, instead of 99 percent, there would be no greenhouse effect on our planet.

But Earth's air contains small amounts of other gases that are greenhouse gases. Most of these occur naturally, and have been a part of our planet's air for billions of years. One is water vapor. Most of Earth's water is in oceans, rivers, lakes, and ice. But a small part of it is carried for a while through the air. It isn't much—but it's important! This water comes down as rain and nourishes everything on the land. It also accounts for much of the Earth's natural greenhouse effect.

Carbon dioxide and methane are two other important greenhouse gases. Like water vapor, they make up only a tiny fraction of the air. Those few molecules of water vapor, carbon dioxide, and methane provide a greenhouse effect that has warmed Earth for billions of years—long before people began to have an impact on its atmosphere. In fact, if there were no water vapor or carbon dioxide in Earth's atmosphere, our planet would be about 33°C (59°F) colder than it is! Earth would be paved in ice—and we wouldn't be here.

By the way, Earth is not the only planet with a greenhouse effect. The air on Mars is very thin, but it is mostly carbon dioxide. The Martian greenhouse effect warms that planet by a few degrees. Venus is a different story. It has a very thick atmosphere that's almost all carbon dioxide. Without its greenhouse effect, Venus would be hot, but livable—about like the Sahara desert. But the greenhouse effect adds almost 370°C (700°F) to its temperature, and makes it the hottest place in our solar system.

Clouds (top), bright ice and dark rock (center), and green plants (bottom) all reflect and absorb sunlight in different ways—and all have an impact on the Earth's climate.

WHAT ELSE WARMS US?

Greenhouse gases have a big effect on Earth's climate. So do the clouds in the sky, the ice on the ground, and even the plants that grow on the land.

Clouds play a huge role in both warming and cooling the Earth. Some cool the planet like giant sun hats by reflecting the Sun's energy and providing shade. But others warm the planet like floating blankets by trapping heat that rises from the ground. High, wispy cirrus clouds don't cast much of a shadow since sunlight passes right through them. But they do a good job of trapping the heat that's trying to escape back to space. So they warm the planet. But down lower to the ground, thick, fluffy cumulus clouds help keep things cool by reflecting sunlight back into space. In today's world, the mix of clouds keeps the Earth a little cooler than it would be if there were no clouds in the sky.

How does the surface of the Earth affect our climate? The sea ice covering the north pole, the huge ice sheets of Antarctica and Greenland, and icy glaciers around the world cover about 10 percent of our planet. White, reflective ice and snow reflect more energy than dark, absorbent land, so the more ice there is, the more of the Sun's energy is reflected back out to space. All this ice keeps Earth cooler than it would be without it.

What about the land? Some things absorb more sunlight than others. You feel this yourself anytime you walk barefoot on a hot summer day. That black parking lot is much hotter on your feet than the white sidewalk. Rocks, dirt, plants, and grass absorb different amounts of sunlight, and reflect the rest.

RIVERS OF AIR

The air doesn't just hover above us. Leaves rustle and flags flutter. Clouds blow across the sky. Our air is constantly flowing around the planet. And it's important that it does. The moving air carries heat from the equator to the poles, and it carries water (in the form of clouds and rain) all around the globe. Where does the energy come from to pump the air around the planet? That energy comes from the Sun. Sunlight warms the oceans and the land. Then the warm surface heats the air just above it. That means the air near the ground is warm—and hot air rises so the air starts to move.

Think of a hot air balloon. You climb into the basket, then turn on a heater that warms the air that fills the balloon. The warm air expands, so it's not as

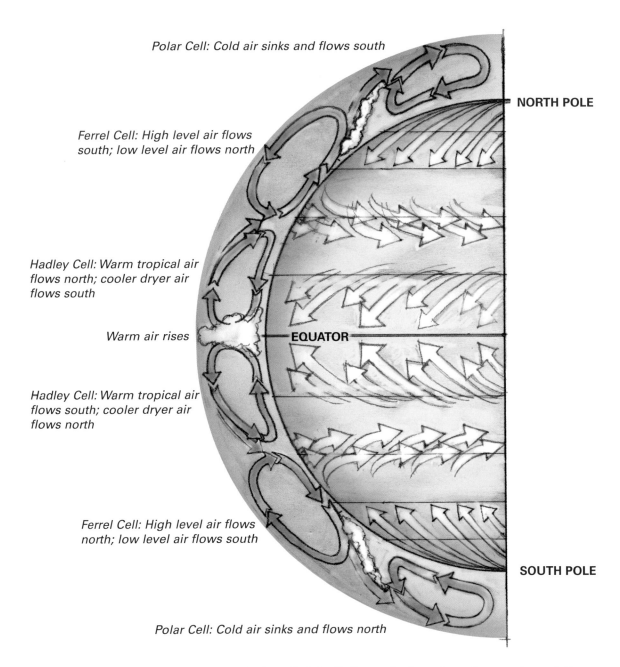

Polar Cell: Cold air sinks and flows south

NORTH POLE

Ferrel Cell: High level air flows south; low level air flows north

Hadley Cell: Warm tropical air flows north; cooler dryer air flows south

Warm air rises

EQUATOR

Hadley Cell: Warm tropical air flows south; cooler dryer air flows north

Ferrel Cell: High level air flows north; low level air flows south

SOUTH POLE

Polar Cell: Cold air sinks and flows north

Air circulation: Huge circulating rivers of air, called "cells," transfer heat from the equator and the tropics, where Earth is warmest, toward the poles.

dense as the surrounding air. That's why it starts to rise, lifting you and the balloon with it.

The air near the equator is warmed by heat from the water below, and begins to rise, like the hot air balloon. Cooler air blows in to replace it, and creates a surface wind. Meanwhile, as the warm air rises, it begins to cool. Several kilometers up it hits a natural lid on the lower atmosphere, and becomes a high-altitude wind. Once the air has cooled, it sinks back toward the ground—but now it's almost 2,000 kilometers from the equator where it started.

Because Earth is shaped like a giant ball, different parts of the planet receive different amounts of sunlight. The Sun shines directly on the part around the equator, but its rays only graze the poles. That's why they're not as warm as the tropics. These temperature differences drive winds in rivers of air that circle the globe. Their directions are influenced by Earth's rotation, and they follow regular patterns that vary with the seasons. Air that's over Japan today will be over the United States in a week; if a huge dust storm kicks dust into the air over Africa, the winds will carry it across the Atlantic Ocean to South America. If a volcano throws ash into the air over the Philippines, winds will carry it across the Pacific to the United States. Most importantly, the moving air redistributes heat around the planet, carrying it from the warm tropics to the chilly poles.

OCEANS IN MOTION

Air is not the only thing that moves around the Earth. The oceans are also in constant motion. The water in the oceans travels on a planet-size conveyor belt from one ocean to another, and from the sunlit surface to the dark sea floor. What drives this enormous conveyor belt? Again, the answer is the Sun. The Sun warms water near the tropics more than that near the poles. Differences in temperature and saltiness send the water flowing around the oceans.

Suppose you could climb into your own personal submarine and dive into the conveyor belt. If you let it take you around the oceans, you'd be in for a very, very long ride. Start your journey with a blob of warm water just off the coast of Florida. You'd travel with it as it flows north up the east coast of the United States. As you head north, the water you were riding with would gradually lose its heat to the air. As it gets colder and colder, the water gets denser and denser. Because salt water freezes at a lower temperature than fresh water, the water **19**

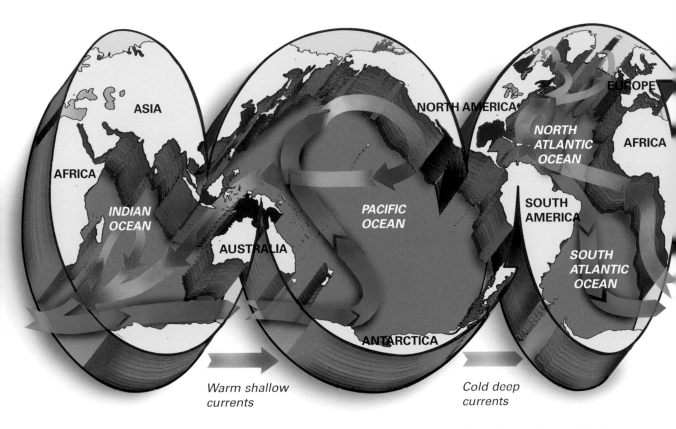

Warm shallow
currents

Cold deep
currents

Ocean circulation: Water in the oceans travels around the Earth and from the surface to the deep ocean like a massive, constantly moving conveyor belt, carrying heat with it. Red arrows show warm water traveling near the ocean surface; blue arrows show cold water traveling through the ocean depths.

can become very cold and still not turn to ice. The cold, salty, dense water sinks before it can freeze.

Eventually, the blob of water you're traveling with is so dense that it sinks like a rock—and you'd have to dive straight down to stay with it. You'd dive all the way to the bottom of the ocean. This cold sinking water is what pulls the conveyor belt. More warm water flows north along the surface to replace it.

Now you're at the bottom of the North Atlantic, about to begin a long, slow journey south. You'd hug the ocean floor with your cold current of water all the way to Antarctica. From there, you would be carried north again into the middle of the Pacific Ocean. The water that you've been traveling with this whole time would slowly warm. As it warmed, it would gradually rise back toward the surface. Several hundred years after you plunged to the bottom, you could finally pop your head out of the sub and feel sunlight again.

But your trip's not over. Winds drag the water west across the Pacific. The tropical Sun warms it even more. Finally, nearly one thousand years after your voyage began, your sub would be back bobbing off the coast of Florida.

This ocean conveyor belt carries the Sun's heat from the equator to the poles. The warm water that flows north toward Europe keeps England much warmer than other parts of the world that are just as far north. It also keeps large parts of the Arctic free of ice.

The circulation of the air and the oceans is critical to our climate and to life on Earth, moving heat from the equator to the poles. But it is not just heat that gets circulated by the air and the oceans. They are also part of Earth's continuous cycles that move water and important elements like carbon around the planet, and this is critical to our climate, too.

A DROP OF WATER

Most of Earth's water—about 97 percent—is in the oceans. Most of the remainder of it is frozen in the massive ice sheets of Antarctica and Greenland. Only a tiny bit of it is in the air. But that tiny bit is important! It's important to the climate as a greenhouse gas. And it's vital to life on Earth—it drifts over land and rains down to provide fresh water for plants, animals, and people.

Let's follow a water molecule as it travels around the planet. Since ninety-seven out of every one hundred water molecules are in the oceans, it's likely that we'd find our molecule there. It would spend a thousand years touring the oceans, passing thermal vents on the sea floor, polar bears in the Arctic, and coral reefs in the tropics. One day, after years of ocean travel, it might finally find itself near the surface basking in the tropical Sun. The sunlight could give it enough energy to break free from the ocean and escape into the air as a gas. Then it would catch the wind and rise high above the waves.

But it better enjoy the view; its stay in the atmosphere would be brief—only a week to ten days. It would rise, and begin to cool. It might huddle closer to other water molecules, joining with some to form a small droplet. That droplet could gather together with other droplets and become a cloud. Soon, some droplets could get big enough to fall back to Earth as rain. Our molecule might

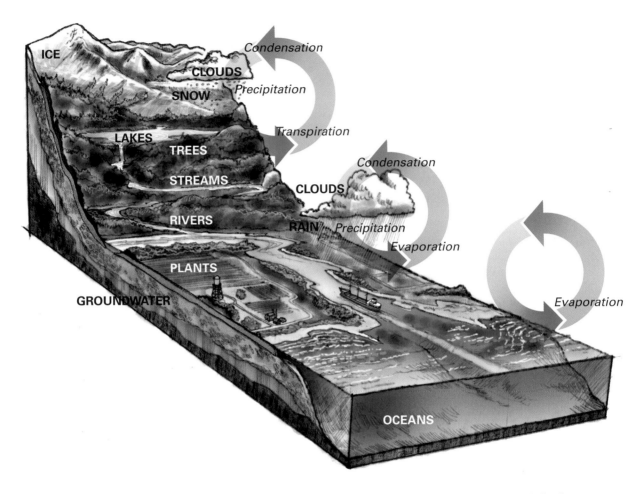

Water circulation: Earth's water is stored in oceans, rivers, lakes, and ice; in the ground, in the atmosphere, and in living things. Water is always on the move. Water evaporates from oceans, lakes, and rivers. Plants take in water from the ground and release water vapor from their leaves (transpiration). Water in the air condenses into clouds and falls as rain, snow, or sleet (precipitation). Rainwater, snow- and icemelt make their way into groundwater or flow downhill to the ocean. Water can spend just days stored as vapor in a cloud—or hundreds of thousands of years locked up as ice in a glacier.

plunk back into the ocean, and begin another long, wet journey on the conveyor belt.

Or the wind might carry it over land. It could fall on a rocky hillside, then trickle down into the soil. There it could find the root of a thirsty wildflower. Once inside the plant, it might be ripped apart by the hungry flower that would use it, along with carbon dioxide, to create a sugar molecule for food (photosyn-

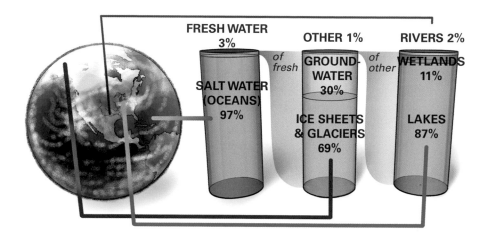

FRESH WATER 3%

OTHER 1%

RIVERS 2%

SALT WATER (OCEANS) 97%

of fresh

GROUND-WATER 30%

ICE SHEETS & GLACIERS 69%

of other

WETLANDS 11%

LAKES 87%

Where is the Earth's water? Most (97%) is in the oceans; only 3% is fresh water. Most fresh water is either in ice sheets and glaciers or underground; only about 1% is in lakes, rivers, and wetlands.

thesis!). Then its life as a water molecule would end—its hydrogen would become part of the sugar molecule, and the flower would exhale its oxygen into the air.

But photosynthesis might not be our molecule's fate. Instead, it might just travel up the stem of the flower, adding strength to the plant. After just a brief visit, it would make its way up to a leaf, and evaporate back into the air.

Perhaps this time it would be blown far north before it fell back to Earth. In the cold, it could condense into a snowflake. It might settle down on a glacier in Greenland. Then it wouldn't melt for a long time. Year after year, snow would fall on top of it. Eventually, it would get packed so close to its neighboring snowflakes that our water molecule would become part of the glacier's ice. As the glacier slowly moves toward the sea, blocks of ice crumble off into the freezing water. Eventually, our molecule would find itself right back in the ocean.

The same water has cycled from the oceans, into the air, and through living things for billions of years. The same is true of all the other important chemicals on Earth, including carbon, nitrogen, and oxygen. Each threads its own route through the oceans, atmosphere, land, and life.

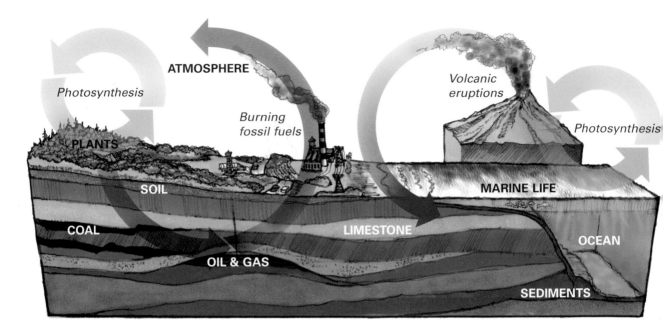

Carbon circulation: Earth's carbon is stored in the atmosphere; in the oceans; in rocks, sediments, and soils; in fossil fuels such as coal and oil; and in living and dead organisms. Carbon circulates in many ways, some of which are shown here. For example, during photosynthesis, plants (and phytoplankton) remove carbon dioxide from the air and store the carbon in their cells. Plants and most other living things return carbon dioxide to the air during respiration. Erupting volcanoes release carbon that has been stored in rocks beneath Earth's surface into the atmosphere. When people burn fossil fuels, carbon from deep underground is released into the air, millions of years ahead of the natural carbon cycle.

CARBON EVERYWHERE

The movement of carbon around the planet is particularly important. In different forms, it plays vital roles in our planet's greenhouse effect, in the chemistry of our oceans, and in the life cycles of all living things.

There's lots of carbon on Earth. Fortunately, it's not all in the atmosphere like it is on Venus. Venus has about the same amount of carbon as Earth, but all of it is in the atmosphere, in the form of carbon dioxide. Venus has no oceans to soak it up, no plants to take it in, and no rain to bring it back to the ground when a volcano sends it into the air. This is why Venus has a huge greenhouse effect.

On Earth, carbon is found in lots of places, but only a tiny bit of it is in the atmosphere. More that 99 percent of our carbon is stored in rocks and ocean sediments, and stays put for millions of years. It eventually makes its way back out, but meanwhile the rest—over four trillion (yes, trillion!) tons of carbon—cycles between the water, air, plants, and animals on the planet. At any one time, you'll find carbon stored in our atmosphere, in our oceans, in our plants, and in our soil.

Let's follow a carbon atom as it travels around the planet. We'll pick one that's part of a carbon dioxide molecule just entering the air—maybe exhaled by a sleeping dog. It would ride the winds for about ten years and travel around the world several times. During this time, it would make its tiny contribution to Earth's greenhouse effect. Then one spring day, it might float into a minuscule hole in a leaf hanging on a tree. It would be carried in a watery stream inside the leaf's veins into a green chloroplast—the part of a cell where photosynthesis takes place. Wham! The carbon dioxide molecule is attacked from all sides by other molecules. First, the oxygen atoms are ripped away from our carbon atom. Then, hydrogen, other carbon atoms, and new oxygen atoms are stuck on. Now our carbon atom is part of a sugar molecule in the leaf.

A hungry mouse might eat the leaf. The sugar in this leafy lunch gives the mouse the energy it needs to scurry around and stay alive. As the mouse digests the leaf, our carbon atom is yanked off the sugar molecule and two oxygen atoms are plunked on it. It's now part of a carbon dioxide molecule again, which the mouse exhales back into the air.

But what if the leaf isn't eaten? It could hang on the tree until fall. Then it will dry up, drop to the ground, and get buried in a pile of leaves. The leaves begin to decay as millions of microbes munch on them. Now our carbon atom is part of the soil. It could stay there for the next fifty years. Eventually, chemical reactions inside a microbe will change it into a carbon dioxide molecule again and it will float away into the air.

This time, the carbon dioxide molecule our atom's riding in might float over the oceans. If it gets close enough to the water it could dissolve in it. It might escape right back out to the air—or it might be taken in by one of the zillions of phytoplankton floating near the sunlit surface. The tiny, single-celled plant would soak up the carbon dioxide molecule—you guessed it, for photosynthesis. Once again, the carbon atom would be ripped away and used to build a sugar molecule.

Now what? A hungry krill might swim by and gulp down the phytoplankton. The tiny shrimplike creature could use the energy from the food to jet away from a hungry whale, and release our carbon atom back into the seawater as carbon dioxide. But it's possible that our atom would remain a part of the krill, maybe in its exoskeleton. When the krill died, its body would slowly sink toward the seafloor, decaying as it drifted down. Our atom might be released back into the water as the krill decays, or it might still be a part of the krill's remains when they settle on the ocean's bottom.

Now our carbon atom could have a very long wait. It might be swept up by the ocean's conveyor belt and make it back up to the surface in only a few hundred years. Or it might get buried under layers of sediment settling down on the ocean floor. Then it would slowly get crushed under intense pressure and heat until it eventually became part of new sedimentary rock—or maybe part of a pocket of oil. Now, part of a fossil fuel, our atom could spend millions of years deep underground. But eventually, it too will return to the surface, lifted by the motion of Earth's tectonic plates.

Earth recycles on a global scale. The precious elements of life—including carbon, water, and oxygen—circulate worldwide. They're carried from pole to pole, from ocean to ocean, and from continent to continent by our oceans and air. They pass through living things to the air, soil, or water—and back again. These cycles connect a thin layer of Earth's water, air, and land as one huge ecosystem—where all living things make their homes. When something disrupts part of a cycle, it affects the whole cycle—and sometimes even the whole planet. Remember our carbon atom, now part of a pocket of oil deep underground? Maybe it will be yanked up out of the ground millions of years ahead of schedule. A deep-sea oil rig could pump it up to the surface. Then it would be processed into gasoline, and pumped into the gas tank of a car. As the car's engine burned the gas, our carbon atom would be ripped away from its molecule and thrown together with two oxygen atoms—part of a carbon dioxide molecule again, heading out of the car's tailpipe and back into the air. Now people have become part of the cycle making changes that can have effects that ripple through everything.

Oil-drilling platforms in the Pacific Ocean off the California coast. Extracting and burning oil and other fossil fuels changes Earth's natural carbon cycle by releasing carbon stored deep underground into the atmosphere millions of years early.

WHAT IN THE WORLD ARE WE DOING?

People are changing Earth's climate. And that's changing the planet in ways we can see and measure. All of Earth is being affected. That means changing conditions and changes for creatures all over the globe.

IT'S GETTING WARMER

It's getting warmer just about everywhere. Over the past fifty years, the temperature has gone up on every continent on Earth. And our air's warming faster now than it was just a few years ago. The last ten years (1997–2007) have been the warmest since 1850—as far back as our temperature records go.

Earth's average temperature has risen about 0.8°C (1.5°F) in the last century. But it's rising faster in some places than others. Since 1980, the mercury's been rising about twice as fast over the continents as over the oceans.

And the temperature's rising faster over some parts of the land than others. The higher latitudes are warming faster than the tropics. In places like New England, average winter temperatures have risen 2.4°C (4.4°F) over the last thirty years. Even farther north, Alaska's average winter temperature has gone up 2.75–4°C (5–7°F) in the past sixty years.

But the increase has been most dramatic at the poles. The warming is amplified there because a lot of the Arctic ice covers an ocean. Once the air started to warm, more sea ice melted during the summer. As it melted, the sunlight that would have hit bright ice hit the dark water instead. The rays that once bounced back out to space heated the water. And, guess what? The warmer water melts the ice even faster. So that patch of the planet got warmer and warmer. This is called positive feedback—when one change brings on even more of that same type of change. It would be as if your heater at home came on automatically on hot days.

The temperature has risen dramatically over Arctic land, too. In Northern Canada, slightly warmer summers have melted more snow and ice, and exposed the ground below. Wildflowers have even started growing. Here, too, sunlight that used to bounce off the snow is now soaked up by the chilly ground. The ground radiates some of that heat into the air—so a little warming leads to more warming, just like over the Arctic Ocean.

THE GREENHOUSE EFFECT

What in the world are we doing that's having such a big effect? We're adding tons and tons and tons of carbon dioxide, methane, and other greenhouse gases

Previous page: February, 2007: A layer of smog hovers over Mexico City.

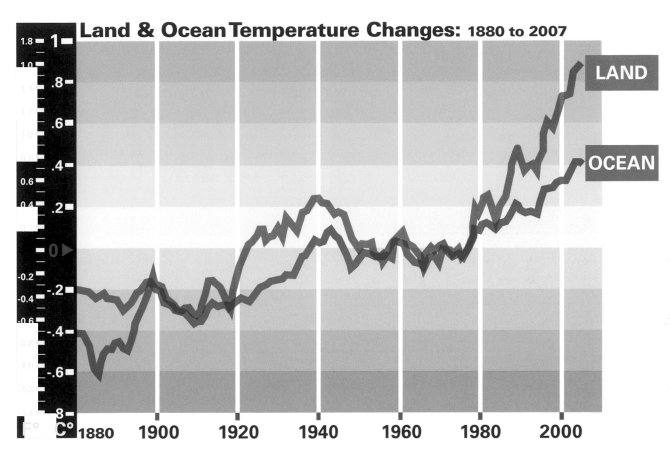

Land & Ocean Temperature Changes: 1880 to 2007

LAND

OCEAN

The change in average global land and ocean temperatures since 1880 (shown on this graph as a difference from the average temperatures for the period 1961-1990). Temperatures have risen sharply over the past 25 years—especially over land, where the increase has been twice as fast as over the ocean.

to the air every day. And since everything on Earth is connected to everything else, the effect is like dropping a stone in the water—the ripples are spreading.

Both carbon dioxide and methane are simple molecules that occur naturally. Carbon dioxide is made of one carbon atom and two oxygen atoms. It's blasted into the sky from deep underground by volcanoes. It wafts into the air during forest fires as trees, which are full of carbon, go up in flames. It's released from decaying plants as microbes digest the dead leaves, stems, and roots. And it escapes from your lungs every time you exhale!

Methane is made of one carbon atom and four hydrogen atoms. It's a very strong greenhouse gas—more effective at trapping heat than carbon dioxide. 31

Fortunately, there's much less of it in the air. It's released from wetlands when dead grass decomposes underwater. In watery environments, where oxygen is scarce, the microbes that chomp on dead plants release methane, not carbon dioxide. Methane is also released from cattle. It's produced in their stomachs as they digest the grass they graze on. Then it's either exhaled or released from the other end of the cow.

These greenhouse gases provide Earth's natural greenhouse effect, and help give us our pleasant climate. They are nothing new: If an alien spacecraft swooped through Earth's atmosphere a million years ago and collected samples of our air to take back to their curious scientists, they would find small amounts of greenhouse gases along with the oxygen and nitrogen.

But now we are adding more of them to the air, and that's adding to the Earth's greenhouse effect and causing the planet to get warmer. That extra warming is already affecting Earth and our life on it.

ADDING TO THE ATMOSPHERE

It's only recently that humans have begun to change the air. Before the 1800s, our civilization had very, very little effect on the atmosphere. But as our numbers grew and our society advanced, that changed in a hurry.

Before 1800, there were fewer than one billion people on Earth. But since then, the world population has skyrocketed. Now there are over 6.5 billion of us sharing our planet. As our numbers have increased, our technology has also advanced. People invented the electric light bulb and the gasoline engine. More and more people began to light their cities, heat their homes and fuel their factories. More and more began to raise cattle, grow rice, and plow fields. People began to travel by car, by ship and by plane. All of these things send greenhouse gases into the air. We're doing more than ever before, and there are enough of us on the planet that it's making a difference.

How have we added carbon dioxide to the air? Some comes from cutting   **33**

down trees. People cut down forests to settle the land and to clear it to grow crops, and they use the wood for fuel and lumber. But all those living trees stored carbon. That carbon is released back into the air when the trees are burned or when they decay.

Most of the rest of the carbon dioxide we emit comes from burning fossil fuels—oil, coal, and natural gas. Fossil fuels are created over millions of years from the ancient remains of living things. The fossils of everything from bushes to buffalo are compressed under layers of rock and sediment. Over the eons, the carbon in the fossils is slowly squeezed into a new form—and eventually turns into coal, oil, or natural gas. Pockets of these "fossil fuels" are trapped underground, under the seafloor or in sediments of ancient rock. We drill for oil and dig for coal, then convert them into forms we can use. When coal is burned in power plants or gasoline made from oil is burned in car engines, the carbon that was once part of a prehistoric plant or animal is released back into the air as carbon dioxide.

We use fossil fuels for everything. Thousands of coal-burning power plants around the world generate the electricity that people use to light their homes and offices and run everything from refrigerators to computers. Oil refineries make the gasoline that fuels the world's cars, trucks, and airplanes. Natural gas is used to heat our homes and cook our food. Fossil fuels are also used in making everything from steel to cement, and from plastics to paper. Our world is built on—and is powered by—fossil fuels.

Carbon dioxide is not the only greenhouse gas that we're adding to the air. Methane is released when oil and coal are extracted from deep underground. It drifts out of landfills as organic material in the trash heap, such as potato peels and apple cores, decay. It also bubbles out of soggy rice paddies, much like it does from wetlands. Rice is eaten by more people in the world than any other grain, and twice as much is grown today than fifty years ago. Methane also comes from cattle. Raising cattle has become big business. Huge herds raised on mega-farms produce the milk we drink and become the beef we eat. Because the number of cows has sky-rocketed, methane belched by cattle has more than quadrupled over the last century.

Year after year, carbon dioxide is piling up in the atmosphere. It enters the air from tailpipes in Texas, Europe, and Japan; from coal plants in Russia, China, and West Virginia; and from deforestation in Brazil, Madagascar, and Washington. Methane wafts out of rice paddies in China, India, and California; and from huge herds of cattle in Texas, Australia, and South America. People around the globe have stepped right in the middle of Earth's carbon cycle.

COUNTING CARBON

How much more carbon dioxide is in the air today than, say, one hundred years ago? That's a great question, because before 1958 no one even knew how much carbon dioxide there was in the air. That year, a young scientist named Charles Keeling developed an instrument that could measure it. He set up a monitoring station near the top of Mauna Loa in Hawaii so that he could analyze samples of fresh air off the ocean.

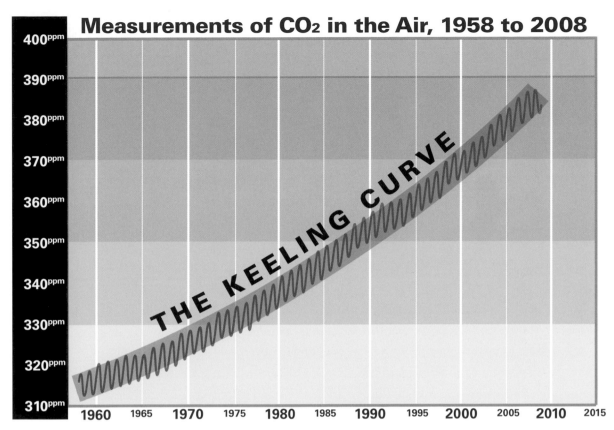

Measurements of CO₂ in the Air, 1958 to 2008

THE KEELING CURVE

400ppm	
390ppm	
380ppm	
370ppm	
360ppm	
350ppm	
340ppm	
330ppm	
320ppm	
310ppm	

1960 1965 1970 1975 1980 1985 1990 1995 2000 2005 2010 2015

Daily measurements taken since 1958 at the Mauna Loa observatory in Hawaii (left), show that the amount of carbon dioxide in the air has gone up every year. In 1958, there were 315 molecules of carbon dioxide out of every one million molecules of air (or, 315 parts per million, called "ppm"). Today, there are almost 385 ppm—an enormous increase in only 50 years. The zigzag line shows how carbon dioxide levels fluctuate with the seasons. Most of Earth's landmass and vegetation are in the northern hemisphere. In the spring and summer, those trees and other plants are growing. They take in carbon dioxide from the air for photosynthesis, so carbon dioxide levels go down. Then in fall and winter many trees drop their leaves and many plants go dormant, so carbon dioxide levels go up.

Keeling's instrument measured the amount of carbon dioxide in the air every day for years. The graph of his measurements has become one of the most famous graphs in science. His data made it clear that the average amount of carbon dioxide in the atmosphere was going up every year. If you climbed to the top of Mauna Loa in 1958 and collected one million molecules of air, 315 of them would have been carbon dioxide molecules. If you made that same trek fifty years later, in 2008, you would find about 385 carbon dioxide molecules in your sample of air. The measurements begun by Keeling continue to this day, and are now being performed at monitoring stations around the world.

37

How important are the changes we're causing? To understand that, scientists needed to understand how Earth's temperature changes naturally. How warm was it 100 years ago? 1,000 years ago? 10,000 years ago? 100,000 years ago?

Temperature records don't go back very far—thermometers have only been around for one hundred fifty years. But clues to the past are everywhere. They're hidden in growth rings of giant redwood trees, in growth rings of coral reefs, in layers of mud on the ocean floor, and deep within Antarctic ice.

Trees keep a logbook of the climate around them. Each year, a tree grows wider, adding another layer around the outside. If you look at a tree stump, you can count the rings and learn the age of the tree. But each ring has more to tell. If the ring is broad, it means that the temperature and amount of rain were just right for the tree to grow. Year after year, trees keep a record that tells us whether they were drenched in rain, basking in the sun, or shivering in the cold. Some of them can take us back a few thousand years.

Scientists have discovered ways to peer even further into the past. Icy mountain glaciers around the world and the huge ice sheets covering Greenland and Antarctica keep frozen records going back tens or even hundreds of thousands of years. These places are so cold that the snow never melts—even in the summer. Each year, a new layer falls on top of the old. As the snow piles up, lower layers get compressed into ice. The ice can be kilometers thick, and digging down into it is like digging back in time.

If you cut out a block of the ice and look at it, you see different layers—a summer layer, then a winter layer, then summer, winter, summer, winter. That's because snow in the summer is different from snow in the winter. In the summer, the temperature is warmer, so the snow crystals are bigger and fluffier. So, you can actually count the years between the bottom of the ice and the top.

Scientists drill deep into the glaciers or ice sheets and pull out long tubes of ice called cores. After a core is labeled, the drill goes deeper into the same hole and pulls out another tube of ice—from even further back in time.

The ice core is like a frozen thermometer. That's because the temperature of years past is recorded in the chemistry of the ice. The oxygen in ice can be one of two types, or isotopes. Both occur naturally, but the amount of one compared to the other is very sensitive to temperature. By determining how much of each there is in a layer of ice, scientists know what the average temperature of the

A team of scientists drill ice cores in Greenland (left). Ice cores stored at the Scripps Institution of Oceanography in San Diego (right) contain a record of Earth's climate over tens of thousands of years.

area was that year. Ice cores have been extracted from glaciers in Alaska, the Himalayas, and the Andes. Scientists have analyzed ice from Greenland that's more than 100,000 years old. They've analyzed ice from Antarctica that's more than 750,000 years old. If those ice cores were laid end to end, they would be several kilometers long! The ice sheet is like a time machine that has transported scientists hundreds of thousands of years into the past.

What do these ice cores tell us? They tell us that a few degrees can make a big difference. The difference between a warm period, like today, and an ice age is only 5 or 6°C!

During the last ice age, enormous glaciers stretched all the way down into the Midwestern United States. About one-third of all the land on Earth was covered by glaciers, and what is Chicago today was buried under kilometers of ice. Our planet was a very different place.

Just a few degrees in Earth's average temperature changes everything. You couldn't live in New York City during an ice age—even the top of the Empire State Building would be buried under a glacier!

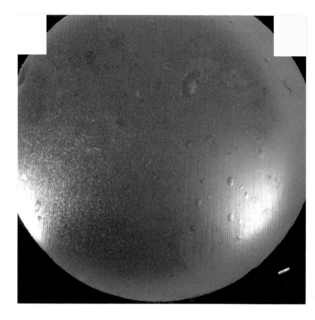

Left: A freshly drilled ice core sample before being removed from a drill.

Right: Trapped bubbles of ancient air visible inside the end an ice core sample.

ANCIENT AIR

The ice cores tell us that Earth's temperature has changed over the eons. What about the carbon dioxide in the atmosphere? Does it change, too? We know from Keeling's famous measurements that it's been rising since 1958. But what about before that?

There's no ancient air around for scientists to study. Or is there? Ah, the ice! It also traps tiny bubbles of air. If you dig deep enough, you'll find ancient air. How do these bubbles form? When snow settles on an ice sheet, there's air between the snow crystals. As the snow gets packed into ice, the air gets sealed in—trapped in small bubbles.

Scientists can study the bubbles encased in the ice cores. Very carefully, they extract the fossil air inside. They know how old that air is because they know how far down it was in the ice. The air in some bubbles is hundreds of thousands of years old.

The ancient air tells us that the amount of carbon dioxide in the atmosphere has also changed over the eons. And it tells us an important thing. There is more carbon dioxide in the air now than there has been in the last million years. A

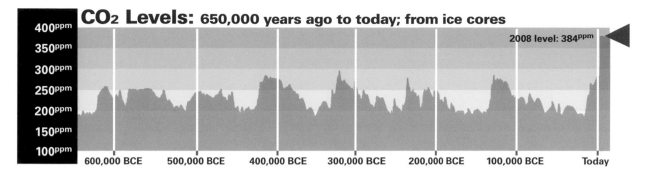

CO₂ Levels: 650,000 years ago to today; from ice cores

400ppm
350ppm
300ppm
250ppm
200ppm
150ppm
100ppm

2008 level: 384ppm

600,000 BCE   500,000 BCE   400,000 BCE   300,000 BCE   200,000 BCE   100,000 BCE   Today

The amount of carbon dioxide in the Earth's atmosphere over the past 650,000 years is shown on this graph. Levels have fluctuated over this period—but carbon dioxide levels in the atmosphere today (shown at the extreme right of the graph) are higher than at any time in at least 650,000 years.

graph of carbon dioxide in the air also shows that temperature and carbon dioxide are linked. When one goes up, so does the other. The message frozen in the ice is this: if the carbon dioxide in the air keeps rising, we should expect the temperature to rise, too.

The extra carbon dioxide and other greenhouse gases we're adding to the air are amplifying Earth's natural greenhouse effect. And that's affecting our climate. Why is that a problem? Every species on Earth has adapted to the temperature, sunlight, and rainfall where it lives. That's why you'll never see a polar bear roaming the beaches of sunny Florida or a saguaro cactus growing in Alaska. But often the inhabitants of an ecosystem are so well adapted to it that even small changes in temperature or rainfall can have drastic effects on them.

What's true for plants and animals is true for people, too. Our entire human civilization has adapted to the climate Earth enjoyed before the extra greenhouse gases began to have an effect. People's lives are based on it, local economies are built on it. The locations of our cities, bridges, and farmlands are determined by it. We grow wheat in Kansas, maple trees in Vermont, and grapes in Northern California because the climates in those parts of the country are just right.

IT'S HAPPENING NOW

Earth's climate is changing—and it's changing now. The evidence is all around. The air and oceans are warming. Earth's ice sheets are melting, sea levels are rising, and storms are more intense. Flowers are blooming earlier. And warming temperatures are nudging plants and animals away from their homes.

Previous page: A polar bear hauls itself onto a chunk of sea ice in the Canadian Arctic. Melting sea ice is threatening the bears' way of life (see page 55).

Moving north: A red fox and a white Arctic fox hunt for food on the same patch of Arctic tundra. With warmer temperatures, the red fox's range is expanding north into areas once hunted only by the Arctic fox.

The evidence is coming in from satellites circling our planet, from computers running sophisticated models of our climate, and from monitoring stations around the globe. Satellites measure deforestation, track migrating species, and analyze the air. They count clouds and record rain around the planet. Computers model Earth's winds, ocean currents, and greenhouse gases. Instruments on mountaintops and ocean piers sniff air, scout seas, and track temperatures worldwide.

Ecologists have trekked through tundra, wetlands, and deserts. Everywhere, nature is struggling with the changes. Many species live in places where even small changes in temperature or rainfall can drastically affect the ecosystem. Maybe one type of plant can't take the change. If it dies, the animals that usually eat it have trouble finding food. And because life is linked in complex webs, what happens to one species always affects others.

SPECIES ON THE MOVE

As an ecosystem gets warmer, the plants and animals that live there have to adapt or move. Many creatures' homes have gotten too warm. They're flying, swimming, or scampering to places where it's cool enough for them to live. Others are venturing beyond their usual neighborhoods to places that were once too chilly for them. Birds. Bushes. Beetles. Bears. All sorts of plants and animals are showing up in places where they've never been.

Robins? In Northern Canada? For the first time, robins are being spotted way up north on Banks Island. This remote, frigid island has been home to the Inuit people for thousands of years. They've walked over its moss-covered tundra for generations. They know every plant and animal on the island. But now there's a stranger in town—the red-breasted robin. The Inuit had never seen a robin before. They didn't even have a name for it. But as the climate warms, the robins are flying farther north in the spring, and the Inuit have a new bird to look at.

In some cases, when one animal moves into a new place, it causes problems for other animals that already live there. Red foxes and Arctic foxes never used to live in the same place. The smaller Arctic fox is made for the frigid climate around the North Pole. Its thick white winter fur blends into the snowy surroundings and covers its body from the tips of its ears to the pads of its paws. It stays warm even in Arctic blizzards. Its larger relative, the red fox, is suited for **45**

Moving up: Pikas live near the tops of high mountains in the western United States. They have a thick fur coat all year around, perfectly designed to keep them warm high in the mountains. But if the temperatures rises above 31°C (88°F) even for an hour they will die. As temperatures get warmer, pikas have to move higher up the mountain to survive—but eventually they run out of space, and now they are disappearing from places where they were once common.

warmer places. But as the Arctic grows warmer, the red foxes have expanded north into territory that once belonged to the smaller white fox. When the two compete for food or living space, the larger red fox usually wins. The little Artic fox is being forced to head farther north.

Some creatures are trekking toward the poles to keep cool, others are inching up mountainsides. If you were to put on a backpack and hike up a mountain, you'd find that the temperature drops about 1°C (1.8°F) for every 100 meters you climb in elevation. The plants and animals you'd see at the bottom would be suited to warmer weather. Then, as you hiked higher, the trees you'd see dotting the mountainside would change and the animals would, too.

The hot, flat Sonoran Desert in Mexico and Arizona is interrupted by mountains jutting up from the desert like ancient pyramids. The mountains are called "sky islands" because they stand alone in the middle of a sea of sand and sage. Each sky island is a layer cake of ecosystems. If you were hiking up Huachuca mountain, every 1,000 feet (300 meters) you'd find a cooler, wetter climate and a different ecosystem. At 2,000 feet, saguaro cactus and rattlesnakes, at 3,000 feet grasslands and leopard frogs, at 4,000 feet juniper trees and shrew. Now as heat invades the sky islands, ecosystems lower on the mountain are inching higher. Eventually, some species may find themselves at the top of a mountain with no place to go. They might adapt, but over time some plants and animals could completely disappear.

When plants and animals are on the move, the diseases that they carry move with them. The diseases can be particularly devastating to others that had not been exposed to them before.

Mosquitoes are slowly inching their way up Mount Kenya. And they're bringing malaria—an often deadly tropical disease—with them. Mosquitoes used to be restricted to the lowlands, where the weather is warmer and there are puddles to breed in. Villages and large cities, like Nairobi, were built farther up the mountain where it was too cold for most insects. People living in these places were safe from the malaria transmitted in a mosquito's sting. Now, the little bloodsucking insects are buzzing higher up the mountain—bringing malaria with them.

WARMER DAYS . . .

In most cold parts of the planet, cold days are not quite as cold as they were a few years ago. Warm days are a little warmer. On any one day, the difference might not seem significant, but those small changes are causing big problems.

Visitors to Yellowstone National Park love to snap photographs of spouting geysers, massive grizzlies, and majestic pines. But lately, Yellowstone's great green forests are turning red. Then they're dying. What's killing the pine trees? Tiny flying beetles.

Usually the beetle population in Yellowstone is kept under control by a cold snap in early fall or late spring. But not anymore. The beetles are infesting trees farther north and higher up the mountains.

Millions of beetles, each no bigger than a grain of rice, swarm a patch of forest. They drill small holes in the pine bark. Then the females burrow into the wood and lay eggs. When the eggs hatch, the larvae tunnel deeper into the tree. The tunnels cut through veins that carry water and nutrients from the roots up to the branches. While the trees slowly turn red and die, countless newborn beetles take to the air to infest nearby trees.

Thousands and thousands of green acres in Yellowstone have gone red. The trees—some hundreds of years old—may stand for a year or so but then they topple to the ground. As the fallen trees decay or burn in wildfires, all of the carbon they've stored as wood is released as carbon dioxide into the air.

The toppled trees also start a domino effect in Yellowstone's ecosystem. As the trees go, so goes an important source of food—pine nuts. The whitebark pine nuts feed birds and squirrels—and grizzly bears. The big bears head to the remote high country in late summer to look for a good place to hibernate. Along the way, they raid underground nests that squirrels have stuffed with pine nuts. The bears fatten up on the nuts to last them through the long winter.

As acre after acre of pine forests are destroyed by the beetles, no one knows what grizzly bears will eat to store enough fat to stay alive while they're hibernating.

. . . AND CHANGING SEASONS

When does spring start? Not when it used to! Along with warmer days, over the past few decades the seasons have begun to shift. Autumn lasts a few days longer. There are fewer frosty nights. Winters are milder. Snow falls a little later in the year and melts a little sooner. Winter clothes are being put away a few days earlier than they were when your parents were young. In Minnesota, ice-skaters have to abandon thawing ice ponds a week earlier. In Georgia, the dogwood trees are flowering several days sooner. Swallows are laying their eggs earlier, and Canadian geese are flying north to their summer homes sooner.

If you hear that your hometown has warmed by 1°C, that doesn't mean that every day is one degree warmer. In most parts of the world, winter and spring have warmed more than summer and fall. Take New England: As the air gets warmer—even a degree or two—there's a little less snow. With less snow around, more sunlight is absorbed by the ground. A little warming leads to more warming.

Dying pine trees turn the hills red in Yellowstone National Park. With warmer temperatures, the tiny pine bark beetle is multiplying and destroying thousands of acres of Yellowstone's once-green forests.

Some of the world's farmers will benefit from the milder weather. But not all of them. People who grow oranges in Florida want a long growing season without frost. But farmers in Kansas who grow winter wheat need some freezing cold days for the plants to flower. They may need to change crops as the Kansas climate warms.

The shorter, milder winters are already affecting maple trees and maple syrup in Vermont. Vermont families started draining sap from maple trees more than two hundred years ago. Their maple syrup has been drizzled over pancakes ever since. But now Vermont's maple trees are being affected by the changing New England climate. To make sap, the trees need several weeks of temperatures below freezing. Once it's made, the sap won't flow unless there's a period of very cold nights with warmer days. For generations, families tapped their trees in early March, then collected sap for about six weeks. But warmer winters have made it necessary to tap the trees earlier. And the season when sap flows is getting shorter. And that means less maple syrup. The climate that suits maple trees is slowly moving north—and so are the maples. By the end of the century, Vermont maple syrup could be a thing of the past. Most maple trees will be in Canada.

Warmer winters in New England might sound like a pleasant change, but it's a problem for the people and the economies of New Hampshire, Vermont, and Maine. There are more warm, slushy winters and fewer cold, snowy ones than there used to be. Less snow means fewer winter vacationers flocking to New England to have fun snowmobiling, skiing, and dog sledding. Now teams of Huskies are pulling golf carts, not sleds. Snowmobile shops are going out of business and ski resorts are opening later and investing in artificial snow.

OUT OF STEP

What tells plants when to bloom and animals when to head to warmer climates for the winter? It's often temperature or sunlight or other signals from the environment. Over generations, each species' pattern of behavior has been perfected to match the behavior of others it depends on. Migrating birds arrive in spring when there is food for them. Flowers bloom when insects are around to pollinate them. But species react differently to climate change. So the inhabitants of an ecosystem can get out of step with each other. It will take time for many species to adjust to the changes. And if they can't, they may disappear.

Salmon are the pride of Seattle—nature's gift to the city's economy. But if waters keep warming in Lake Washington, where young salmon grow up, the salmon and the industry they spawned could be in trouble. Tiny animals called zooplankton used to multiply at the same time that green algae bloomed in the lake. The zooplankton thrived by gobbling up the algae. But now the surface of the lake is warmer. The algae have happily adapted—they're blooming earlier in

Sockeye salmon, Lake Washington

spring. But the zooplankton haven't adapted. Now the two species are out of sync, and not as many zooplankton are surviving. This is big trouble for young salmon. They need to eat lots of zooplankton to grow strong before they swim downstream to live in the ocean. And trouble for the salmon means trouble for Seattle's fish markets and restaurants.

Some birds are struggling to keep up with the shifting seasons, too. Songbirds called great tits nest in oak trees all over Europe. They lay their eggs so they'll hatch at the same time as caterpillars are crawling over the oak branches and feeding on oak buds. But now, the oaks are budding earlier in the spring. The caterpillars have adapted and are coming out twenty days sooner. Some individual birds in Sweden and elsewhere have updated their calendars and are laying their eggs earlier. But most great tits are still laying their eggs by the old calendar. Now when the chicks break out of their shells, there's not much for them to eat. In some places, such as The Netherlands, the numbers of these songbirds are way down.

Warming days and changing seasons affect not only living things, but also ice sheets, icebergs, and glaciers. Ice covers about 10 percent of our planet. As Earth's air warms, the ice is melting. Drip by drip, our ice sheets, sea ice, and mountain glaciers, are thawing. And that in turn is affecting people, plants, and animals in many parts of the world.

Glaciers are giant rivers of ice. They form in mountain valleys, and are so heavy that they flow under their own weight. Ice accumulates on a glacier when the weather is cold, and some melts when the weather is warmer. A glacier's long-term survival depends on the balance between the build-up of snow in the winter and the melting in the summer. Glaciers can be found around the world—in the Himalayas in Asia, the Andes in South America, and the Alps in Europe. Now glaciers on every continent are shrinking. In some cases, they've even disappeared. They've melted away. Even Glacier National Park in the United States is losing the very thing it was named for. When the park opened a century ago, it was home to 150 glistening glaciers. Today only 27 are left. Scientists predict the last of the park's glaciers will be gone by 2030.

Why should people care about glaciers? Because glaciers are like giant water coolers. In the summer, the taps open and melt water fills many of Earth's major rivers.

Thousands of glaciers high in the Himalayas store much of Asia's water supply. In the thin air more than 13,000 feet above sea level, the sound of water gurgling underground means a glacier is melting from inside. The water empties out of the glacier's snout. It rushes downhill to fill mighty rivers like the Yangtze, Mekong, and Ganges. Each begins high in the Himalayas and carries water to the lowlands below. More than a billion people depend on these rivers for water to drink, water to irrigate their crops, and flowing water to generate their electricity. And they depend on the glaciers high up in the Himalayas to keep these rivers flowing.

At first, as these glaciers melt, more water than usual will fill the rivers. In some places, the banks will overflow and flood the low-lying lands. The unwelcome water will drown crops and submerge villages in India, Bangladesh, and China. But over time, as the store of ice disappears, the glaciers will no longer feed the rivers. This could be a catastrophe for one-sixth of the world's population.

A meltwater stream rushes downhill from the mountains of northwestern Pakistan. Glaciers in the Himalayas and other mountain ranges are the source of water for hundreds of millions of people.

A satellite image of the Jakobshavn glacier in Greenland showing the location of the glacier's edge. Since 2000, the edge of the glacier has retreated quickly—sometimes as much as 100 feet per day.

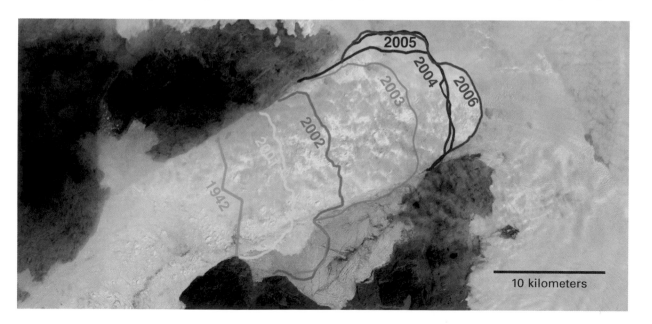

A MELTING OCEAN

There's no land at the North Pole, just water. But that water is covered by ice—the white polar cap that tops our planet. The Arctic ice cap is a shifting pack of sea ice floating on the Arctic Ocean. During the winter the ice pack grows to the size of the United States. It shrinks to about half that size in summer. When explorers first trekked to the North Pole, dogs pulled their sleds hundreds of miles over a crust of sea ice that was several meters thick. But future explorers may have to make the trip by boat. Before too long, the Arctic Ocean could be ice-free in the summer.

The Arctic teems with life, from its largest predators, the killer whale and polar bear, to small birds like the Arctic tern. The warmer weather is affecting the polar animals who have depended on the sea ice for centuries.

Polar bears use the chunks of frozen ocean as stepping stones to hunt down seals that swim near shore. The big white bears stalk their prey and then wait by the edge of the ice for a seal to pop up for air. Without the sea ice, the bears couldn't get near the fast-swimming seals. Now, as sea ice breaks up earlier, they have less time to hunt for seals. The bears' way of life is threatened. In some places, they're adapting by eating other food—like snow geese—but their long-term survival is linked to the sea ice.

Shrinking sea ice is changing life in the Bering Sea, too. This sea off the coast of Alaska bustles with krill and fish, whales and walruses, seals and seabirds, and clams and crabs. Part of the Bering Sea freezes each winter. The translucent ice lets sunlight through, so algae can grow on the bottom of the ice. Today the water is warmer, so less sea ice forms. That means there's less ice algae—and less food for the clams and amphipods sitting on the seafloor. These bottom-dwellers can't move; they depend on the algae sinking down to them. Without a steady source of food, populations of clams and amphipods have dwindled.

This in turn has an impact on other species. Normally gray whales prepare for their winter migration to warmer waters by feasting on amphipods that carpet the floor of the Bering Sea. But lately when the whales dive to scoop up mouthfuls of their favorite food, they're coming up hungry. The whales swimming south are skinnier and have less blubber under their skin than usual.

Facing page: This meltwater stream started as a trickle. Now it cuts deep into the Greenland ice sheet.

Ice algae stains the underside of floating pack ice green-yellow (left). Ice algae is the beginning of the Arctic ocean food chain that eventually feeds gray whales like this one (right), shown feeding on the bottom of the North Pacific Ocean.

Marine biologists are seeing signs that these gentle giants are slowly adapting by switching to other food.

People who live in the towns and villages that rim the Arctic Ocean are feeling the changes, too. Shishmaref is a small village on Alaska's northwest coast. Thick ice once protected the shore from the crashing waves of stormy seas, but now much of that ice is gone. Ferocious waves pound the shoreline and eat away at the land. Many of the homes and buildings in this small village are in danger of tumbling into the sea. The people of Shishmaref have to pack up and move their whole village farther from the rough water. They, and other Alaskan villagers along the battered coast, are among the world's first climate refugees.

SHRINKING SHEETS OF ICE

There is a lot of ice in Earth's glaciers and sea ice. But most of Earth's ice is locked up in the gigantic ice sheets that cover Greenland and Antarctica.

Greenland's ice sheet would fit over the Eastern United States from the

Shishmaref, Alaska: A house tips over, destroyed by beach erosion. Rising temperatures have caused a reduction in sea ice, making this Arctic town's beaches vulnerable to erosion.

Atlantic Ocean to the Mississippi River. The ice sheets covering Antarctica are even bigger. Ninety percent of the world's ice lies on top this huge continent that covers the South Pole. It's almost completely hidden under a blanket of ice that's about 2 kilometers thick and 1.5 times the size of the United States.

Now those ice sheets are shrinking. Each year, they grow a little when snow falls, and shrink a little when ice around their edges breaks off into the sea. When the growing and shrinking are in balance, the ice sheets stay about the same size. This is not the case today: New ice is not forming fast enough to keep up with the shrinking of the giant ice sheets.

Scientists thought they knew how to estimate the effects of warming on the ice sheets. If you've dropped an ice cube on a kitchen table, you know that when the ice is exposed to warmer air it starts to melt. The water pools on the table, and eventually drips onto the floor. Until recently, scientists assumed that the ice sheets shrank in the same way: The tops would melt, and the water would run off into the ocean. They estimated that it would take thousands of years for them to melt—even if the Earth warmed several degrees.

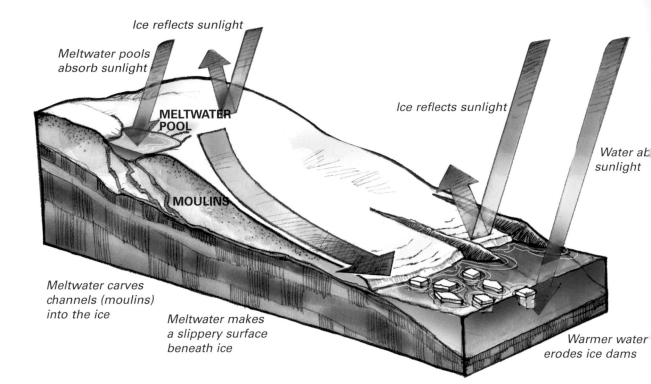

Ice reflects sunlight

Meltwater pools
absorb sunlight

Ice reflects sunlight

MELTWATER POOL

Water ab
sunlight

MOULINS

Meltwater carves
channels (moulins)
into the ice

Meltwater makes
a slippery surface
beneath ice

Warmer water
erodes ice dams

Cross-section of an ice sheet, showing how several factors can work together to speed up ice loss.

But in the last few years, ice sheets have been shrinking faster than scientists expected. Apparently, they're not just melting like ice cubes. The glaciers that guard the edges of ice sheets are flowing faster toward the water, and the huge ice shelves that hang out over the water are crumbling into the sea. Scientists studying the ice sheets have discovered some things that they hadn't thought of.

Puddles of melted ice can cut through cracks and crevices in the ice and tunnel all the way to the ground. This water lubricates the ground, and makes it easier for the glaciers to slide toward the ocean.

Warmer seawater is also speeding up the loss of ice. Glaciers along the coasts are often held in place by walls of ice hundreds of meters high that reach up from the seafloor to anchor the glaciers to the land. Now the warmer water weakens the ice walls, eating away at the fortress that keeps the glacier from flowing. Once the walls are gone, the glaciers slip slide toward the sea.

In Greenland, some glaciers are flowing toward the sea twice as fast as they were only a few years ago. Scientists now fear that the ice sheets could be gone in a few centuries, not a few millennia.

 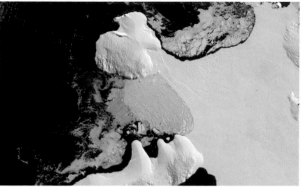

In March 2008, scientists observed the breakup of a huge piece of the Antarctic ice shelf. The image on the left, taken from a satellite, shows intact white ice and a clear boundary between the ice and the dark ocean. In the image on the right, taken eighteen days later, solid ice has been replaced by a blue-white jumble of broken blocks of ice that have collapsed into the ocean. As the shelf collapsed, scientists flew over it and took photographs of a huge crack opening in the surface of the ice (below).

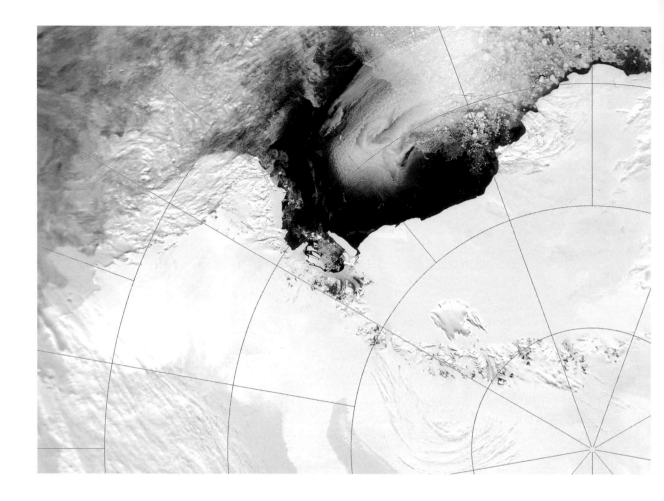

If you live near a sunny beach in Florida, you may not care that ice sheets and the glaciers that guard them are melting. But you should! As they melt, torrents of fresh water are pouring into the world's oceans. It's just like adding water to a bathtub—the water level is going to rise. If it rises too much, your favorite beach just might disappear.

Antarctica may be the world's coldest continent, but all kinds of hardy creatures live there. Some of them make their homes along the edge of the ice sheets. But most live in the Southern Ocean—on sea ice or in the water that surrounds Antarctica. Mosses in wet sand and lichens on chilly rocks eek out life and provide food and shelter for tiny worms and mites. Gulls and terns swoop in for dinner and to rest on their way home to nearby islands. Penguins and seals come and go between the icy water and the icy shore. And the ocean is packed with life—algae and plankton, ice fish and cod, dolphins and whales.

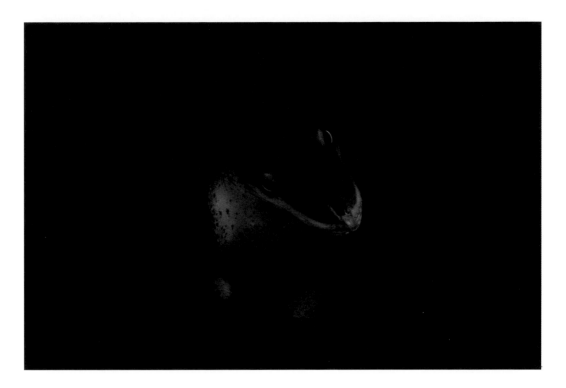

Facing page: A vast cloud of phytoplankton appears as a green stain in the cold Ross Sea off the Antarctic coast in this satellite picture. These tiny plant-like organisms are the first link in many ocean food chains—and are very sensitive to changes in water temperature. Changes at the bottom of the food chain can reach all the way to the animals at the top—like this leopard seal (above).

Like phytoplankton, algae are the basis of many ocean food chains. Small shrimplike animals called krill eat both. When phytoplankton are scarce, krill swim upside down and scrape algae off the bottom of the sea ice. But as the ice disappears, so does the ice algae. This means fewer krill survive. Guess whose favorite meal is krill? Emperor and Adélie penguins. These penguins like to float on rafts of sea ice and dive into the water to scoop mouthfuls of krill. Lately, they're getting more salt water than krill.

While some species lose, others win. Salps are small sea creatures that look like transparent pickles. As the Southern Ocean warms and sea ice melts, salps are floating farther south toward Antarctica. They feed on phytoplankton, and are multiplying like crazy. But their good fortune has unraveled the food chain. They're eating so much phytoplankton there's not enough left for the krill. The waters are now brimming with salps—but there are not many krill left. This means more problems for penguins, which don't eat salps.

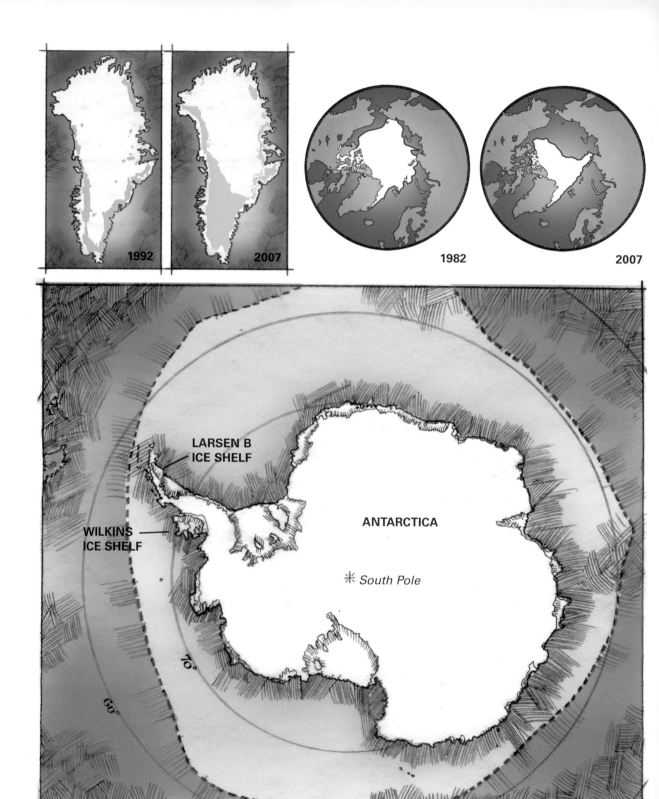

1992

2007

1982

2007

LARSEN B
ICE SHELF

WILKINS
ICE SHELF

ANTARCTICA

✳ *South Pole*

70°

60°

Facing page: The shaded portions of the two images of Greenland (top left) show areas of above-average melting of the ice cap during summer—and how the amount of melting has grown between 1992 and 2007. The two images of the North Pole (top right) show the decrease in the amount of sea ice covering the Arctic Ocean between the summers of 1982 and 2007. In the Antarctic (bottom), scientists observed the breakup of large areas of the Larsen B Ice Shelf in 2002 and the Wilkins Ice Shelf in 2008.

BOGGY UNDERFOOT

Unless you live in Alaska, Canada, or Siberia, you've probably never walked on permafrost. But this frozen ground covers one-fourth of the land on Earth, most of it in the frigid north, just below the Artic circle.

What is permafrost? And why should we care that it starting to thaw?

Permafrost is permanently frozen ground. One type, called "loess," covers more than one million square kilometers of Siberia. Loess is frozen soil that accumulated during the last ice age. Our planet was drier then, and high winds blew dust thousands of kilometers. The dust carried bits of roots and grass. As they settled over the frozen land, some took hold and began to grow. But not for long—they froze, too. Then the howling winds deposited another layer of dust over them. After thousands of years, this icy soil full of frozen roots and shoots became very thick. And all the carbon in the frozen pieces of plants has been locked in the loess for more than ten thousand years!

But over the last twenty-five years, the top of the loess has warmed and started to thaw. As it thaws, the frozen grasses finally decay. If they're exposed to oxygen, the microbes that attack them release carbon dioxide. If they're below ground with no oxygen around, other microbes digest them and release methane.

This is another example of how a little warming can lead to more warming. The warmer air thaws the permafrost, so the permafrost releases greenhouse gases, and those greenhouse gases increase the planet's greenhouse effect and lead to even more warming. A lot of carbon is stored in the loess. If all of it thawed and all of the plant bits in it decayed, the greenhouse gases in the air would more than double.

Other types of permafrost don't hold as many frozen plant pieces as loess, but the thawing can still cause problems. The soil in parts of Alaska and Canada has started to warm—and the impact is dramatic for the people who live there. The ground used to be frozen hard. Homes and roads were built on it. Trees **63**

Fairbanks, Alaska: Thawing permafrost has caused big bumps in this bicycle path.

grew in it. Oil pipelines were constructed along it. Now in some places the ground is soft and squishy. Walking on it is like walking on a soggy trampoline. Trees are tilting, wobbling, and falling. Homes are sinking. The people of Newtok, Alaska, live on the edge of the Bering Sea. Not only is the sea ice that used to protect the shore melting, but the ground the town was built on is thawing! Newtok could be gone in a few years. The entire village will soon have to move to more solid ground.

UNEVEN RAINS

The warmer the air gets, the more water evaporates from the oceans, lakes, and rivers and the more is sucked from plants and soils. That water floats into the air and becomes part of our weather. But water only stays in the atmosphere for a few days—the water cycle brings it right back down to Earth. So more water in the air means more rain and more snow.

Scientists have discovered that the rainy parts of our planet are getting even more rain and the drier places are getting even less. They've learned this by measuring rainfall over land and also, oddly enough, the saltiness of the oceans. How does the saltiness of the oceans tell us about rainfall? Imagine a hot, sunny day off the coast of Mexico. The heat evaporates water—fresh water—out of the ocean and leaves the salt behind. So the ocean becomes a little saltier.

Now imagine the ocean near a tropical island. Yes, water evaporates there, too. But frequent summer rainstorms drop lots of fresh rainwater back in. This dilutes the seawater and makes it a little less salty. The oceans are becoming saltier in some places than in others. By measuring how the saltiness changes, scientists can tell where it's raining more, like the tropics, and where it's raining less.

Of course rainfall amounts are changing over land, too. Places with rainy climates are getting even more rain, and deserts are getting even less. Wet places like the East Coast of the United States, Northern Europe, and Northern Asia have gotten much wetter. And dry places like the Sahel Desert and other deserts in Africa, Europe, and the United States have gotten even drier.

Temperatures in the desert mountains of California have climbed and rainfall has dropped. The scorpions, prairie dogs, and coyotes are used to blazing heat and scarce water, but now the conditions are more extreme. Shrubs are disappearing and water is harder to find. Bighorn sheep have lived in these rugged foothills and craggy canyons for thousands of years. But as warmer air bakes the parched land, even they are having a hard time.

The forests of Northern Arizona have also gotten warmer and drier. The mix of trees used to be about half junipers and half piñon pines. But extended drought has weakened the piñon pines. They have been attacked by bark beetles and many have died. Junipers can withstand drought more easily, so now swaths of forest are all juniper. This has rippled thorough the rest of the ecosystem—now piñon mice and several other creatures are scrambling to find new homes.

Because there's more water in the clouds, rainstorms everywhere are more intense. This is not good news for places that already get a lot of rain. When torrential rain pounds ground that is already saturated, there's nowhere for the water to go. It floods fields, farms, and city streets. But violent rainstorms are not good for deserts either. Yes, they need the rain. But when it all comes down at once, it sweeps through the desert in flash floods. The water just rushes off the land that needs it so badly.

WARMER WATER

The air isn't the only thing that's getting warmer. About 80 percent of the heat trapped by the extra greenhouse gases in the atmosphere has been soaked up by the oceans.

Oceanographers have compiled millions of temperature readings from ocean buoys, research ships, and piers. They've learned that the average temperature of the world's oceans has risen .04°C (.07°F) in just the last fifty years. That sounds like very little. But more than 70 percent of our planet's surface is deep oceans, so it adds up to a lot of heat. If all that heat had stayed in the air instead of going into the oceans, the air today would be 22°C (40°F) hotter than it is! A pleasantly warm afternoon would be sizzling hot.

Because sunlight is absorbed at the ocean's surface, the water near the surface is much warmer than the water deeper down. You can feel this next time you go swimming. The top of a pool or lake is much warmer than water down by your feet.

Since the oceans and the atmosphere influence each other a lot, you might expect this to influence our weather. It does. Perhaps the most dramatic effect is on hurricanes. Hurricanes get much of their energy from the warm water of the tropics. They won't form at all if the surface temperature is less than 26°C (79°F). But the more it rises above that critical temperature, the more intense a hurricane can get. Atmospheric scientists have analyzed the hurricanes that formed in the Atlantic ocean during the last century. They've found that on average, there are twice as many hurricanes today as there were one hundred years ago, and that today's hurricanes are more intense.

August 28, 2005: Hurricane Katrina crossing the Gulf of Mexico, before making landfall near New Orleans. With warming ocean temperatures, storms are likely to become more intense.

Temperature also has an effect on sea level. That's because water expands when it's heated. The water molecules move faster and spread farther apart so the water takes up more room. This happens every time you heat water in the kitchen, too. So as the oceans warm up, sea levels around the world are rising. They're now rising about 3 millimeters each year. About half of that is just due to the warmer, expanding water. The rest is the result of more water pouring into the oceans from melting glaciers and ice sheets. Tide gauges on piers and, more recently, laser radars on satellites show that the seas are about 15–20 centimeters (6–8 inches) higher than they were a century ago.

Rising sea levels threaten low-lying islands and coastal areas around the world, such as the islands of Tuvalu in the Pacific Ocean, all of which lie less than 16 feet above sea level.

Monterey, California: Tube snails like these have moved into Monterey Bay from the south as water temperatures have increased.

Rising waters could chase millions of people from coastal villages, towns, and even cities around the world. Small Pacific island nations like Tuvalu could be swallowed by the sea. Tuvalu's winter tides are now higher. Beaches are eroding. Waves are crashing over roads and washing into homes and coconut groves. Well water is spoiled—it's too salty to drink. On some islands, people have been evacuated to higher ground. But as oceans creep higher, many islanders will be forced to pack up their belongings and move to someplace else.

It isn't just people that lose their homes when sea levels rise. Plants and animals in river delta ecosystems from the Nile to the Ganges to the Mississippi are losing theirs, too. The Mississippi River delta is the largest wetlands in the United States, and a thriving salt marsh ecosystem. But each year, up to 120 square kilometers of the wetland erodes and sinks into the Gulf of Mexico. The delta sinks naturally anyway, but now the rising gulf waters are eating away at it, too. The disappearing delta disrupts the lives of pelicans, crayfish, and alligators and squeezes them into a smaller home.

What about life in the ocean? Have fish, plankton, and crustaceans noticed that the thermostat's going up? The answer is yes. Monterey Bay in northern California is famous for its tide pools. It's a popular place, packed with seaweed, snails, barnacles, sea stars, and crabs. At high tide, waves crash over the rocks and fill the tide pools with cool, salty water. Sea life clings to the rocks to keep from washing away in the waves. At low tide, some hide in the shade of rocks and some curl up in their shells to keep from drying out in the Sun.

In the 1930s, a marine ecologist painstakingly identified all the species living in the bay's tide pools. That was a while ago, and since then the bay has warmed. A few years ago, a small tube snail started showing up on the rocks. The snail is common farther south, but it had never been spotted in Monterey Bay. As the water off the Pacific coast got warmer, the little snail migrated north. Apparently many other animals had the same idea. When scientists repeated the cataloging of creatures, they discovered that life in the tide pools had changed. Some species, including the tube snail, had moved in from the south. Others that prefer cooler conditions, including a crab and two sea stars, had moved out—presumably making their homes farther up the coast.

The oceans are so big and so deep that it takes a long time for them to change even a little—so most sea creatures are used to living within a small range of temperatures. Some are extremely sensitive to temperature. They're threatened as the water around them warms. Phytoplankton, the microscopic plants that are the first link in most ocean food chains, are a very important example. These minuscule green microbes ride the waves in all the world's oceans, soaking up carbon dioxide from the water for photosynthesis. Day in and day out, countless phytoplankton pull tons and tons of carbon dioxide from the oceans, making it possible for the water to absorb more from the overloaded air.

Phytoplankton multiply like crazy in a cool ocean. In fact, when the conditions are right, giant green blooms of zillions of the tiny plants can even be seen from space. But in recent years, there are far fewer of them in some oceans. The water's too warm. This means trouble for sea life higher up the food chain, from krill and fish to seals and seabirds. And fewer phytoplankton also means more carbon dioxide stays in the surface water, which means less gets pulled from the air into the water. Phytoplankton have a big affect on the amount of carbon dioxide in the air!

Another creature that is ultra-sensitive to temperature is coral—the tiny animal responsible for building coral reefs in tropical waters around the world.

The Great Barrier Reef off the northeastern coast of Australia is gigantic. This amazing ecosystem is more than 1,000 miles (1,610 km) long. But it was built over thousands of years by generations of little corals, each no bigger than a pencil eraser. A tiny coral starts life swimming through the water until it finds a rock to cling to. Eventually thousands and thousands of other corals make their home on the same rock, and huge colonies are formed.

Corals take in calcium and carbonate, a molecule made of carbon and oxygen, from seawater. Then they turn them into limestone—also called calcium carbonate—to make their hard, rocky skeletons. Each coral builds a skeleton around its soft body, like a suit of armor. The coral sits in its stony suit protected from hungry predators and stormy seas. At night, it sticks its mouth out into the water to capture food.

Living corals make up the outer layer of a coral reef. As the reef slowly grows, all sorts of sea creatures move in and make their homes in the reef's countless cracks, crevices, and caves. The Great Barrier Reef is home to nearly a million different kinds of fish, crabs, eels, plankton, sponges, sea urchins, sea turtles, octopuses, dolphins, and others.

Coral reefs are splashed with color. But the tiny corals themselves are a chalky white. They get their color from algae living inside their cells. The coral

Colorful living coral surrounds a head of coral bleached gray-white by rising water temperatures off the coast of Indonesia.

provides the algae with a safe place to live. The algae provide the coral with food and oxygen from photosynthesis. If corals are stressed, for example if the waters around them become too warm, they kick out their colorful algae tenants. Suddenly the colony turns chalk white. This is called "coral bleaching." It's really just the natural color of corals' skeletons, but it's a sign that the corals are in trouble. Sometimes they can recover and get back the algae they depend on. But if the water stays too warm, the coral will die. And without a healthy coral reef, the whole ecosystem will collapse.

Left: Coral heads in the ocean near Indonesia, bleached almost entirely white as a result of changes in ocean temperature.

Right: A pteropod, or sea butterfly. Experiments have shown that the sea butterfly's shell will dissolve with an increase in the acidity of the ocean to the level predicted by the end of the century.

Today, warmer oceans threaten many of these colorful underwater colonies. Even though corals live in warm tropical waters, an increase of only one or two degrees can be enough to affect these fragile animals.

MORE ACIDIC OCEANS

Everywhere the air meets the ocean, a swap takes place. Carbon dioxide in the air dissolves into the water while carbon dioxide in the water bubbles into the air. Over the eons, a balance is reached.

Over the past two centuries, as the level of carbon dioxide in the air has been rising, more and more of it has been going into the oceans. The oceans have soaked up one-half of the carbon dioxide that people have put into the air. For a while, scientists thought this was a good thing—it might slow down the warming from the boosted greenhouse effect. But while the ocean's ability to take in carbon dioxide has slowed the build up of greenhouse gases in the atmosphere, it's caused problems in the oceans themselves. All that extra carbon dioxide is changing the chemistry of the oceans. It's making them more acidic.

The acidity of the ocean is kept in check by certain carbon-carrying molecules that neutralize any acid they come across. This natural process has kept the acidity of the ocean stable for eons. But today it can't keep up with all the carbon dioxide pouring into the ocean—the process is on overload.

How does this common gas—the same one you drink in every soda and exhale in every breath—cause trouble in the ocean? When carbon dioxide dissolves, it reacts with water to form carbonic acid. This is the acid—carbon dioxide in disguise—that is making the oceans more acidic. They are only a little bit more acidic. But it's enough that sea life—from corals to sea snails to phytoplankton—is finding it harder to build their protective shells and skeletons. These animals need carbonate to build their shells and skeletons, and as the oceans become more acidic, there is less carbonate around because it's soaking up all the extra acid. For shell-building creatures it's like trying to build a brick house with just bricks and no mortar to glue them together.

The oceans are enormous. There's so much water in them that they're very hard to change. But we're changing them. And these changes will be very difficult to reverse. Already, they are affecting the phytoplankton that are the heart of most ocean food chains and help control the carbon dioxide in the air, coral reefs that are home to more species of sea life than any place else in the oceans, and countless plants, animals, and people living along the coasts of every continent.

The signs of our changing climate are all around us. Winds and waves are warmer. Ten-thousand-year-old glaciers are melting. Seas are creeping farther up beaches. Seasons are different. And from the north pole to the south pole, and every place in between, people, plants and animals are trying to keep up with all the changes.

WHAT'S NEXT?

Even if people stopped sending greenhouse gases into the air tomorrow—if everyone stopped driving cars, turning on lights, and making things—Earth would keep changing. The greenhouse gases we've already added will continue to affect our climate for many years to come. The temperature of the air will keep climbing. And like a warm whisper, this will affect the rest of the planet.

What will the planet be like in twenty years? In fifty years? Scientists could borrow a crystal ball to peek into the future. Instead, they've made their own.

Scientists have written very complex computer programs to simulate Earth and its climate. That's no small job. The programs have to include the warming by the Sun, the circulation of the air, the currents in the oceans, the effect of greenhouse gases, and everything else that makes Earth, well, Earth—from phytoplankton and rainforests to ice sheets and permafrost, and from wind and rain to clouds and cows.

These computer programs are run by the fastest, most powerful computers on Earth. They start with conditions on our planet today. Then they step forward in time, solving the equations to describe what the world will be like next year, ten years, fifty years, one hundred years into the future.

But computer calculations are only as good as the information that scientists put in. The early computer models didn't even include plants! As scientists learn more, they improve the models. But there's still lots of room for improvement.

For example, it's not easy to estimate how much methane is going into the air. How much comes out of rice paddies around the world? Out of all the cows on the planet? Out of the thawing permafrost? It's also hard to predict how fast chunks of glaciers and ice sheets will break off and disappear into the sea.

And those pesky clouds are a problem, too. Clouds are small and constantly changing. Today's computer models just can't predict how they will act. As the world warms, there might be more clouds in the sky—or fewer. There might be mostly clouds that warm the planet—or mostly clouds that cool it.

But computer models are getting better all the time. These sophisticated programs are slowly bringing the future into focus. What do these high-tech crystal balls predict?

Through this century, temperatures will keep going up. The warming will follow the same trends we're already seeing. The biggest changes will be over land and in the northern parts of the planet. There will be less snow on the ground, and less ice in the ocean. Permafrost will get soggier and soggier. There will be more heat waves. Hurricanes will pack stronger winds and rains. Sea levels will inch higher. Oceans will become warmer and more acidic.

But how much will our planet change? The computers can't tell us—because they're missing one critical piece of information: What will the people of the world decide to do about greenhouse gases? Will we continue along the same

Crowds enjoy a hot day in New York City's Central Park. What people decide will determine our future climate—and the future of our planet.

path, using more and more energy and getting most of it from fossil fuels? Or will we decide it's time to change?

Greenhouse gases loft into the air from tailpipes in the United States and China, from factories in Russia and Australia, and from rice paddies in India and California. One country can't solve this problem by itself. We all need to think and act differently. This is a global challenge that requires global action.

It's hard to imagine a world without coral reefs, tropical forests, or Arctic ice, but it could happen. It's up to all of us to preserve this special planet we call home.

SOURCES/ RESOURCES

The study of Earth's climate is complex, dynamic, and rapidly evolving—new findings are released almost every day. It involves thousands and thousands of scientists around the globe from every walk of science—biology, chemistry, physics, mathematics, and engineering as well as cross-disciplinary fields like oceanography, ecology, geophysics, and meteorology. It involves teams of scientists, with different science backgrounds, working together to unravel the details of how people are reshaping the climate and how this is impacting everything from the weather to the web of life.

We used a wide variety of resources in writing this book. A few, however, proved especially helpful—informative, insightful, and clearly written. We recommend these resources for students, educators, librarians, and parents seeking to learn more about this important topic.

Climate Change 2007, the most recent United Nations Report of the Intergovernmental Panel on Climate Change (IPCC). This "Synthesis Report" summarizes three separate reports that provide the current state of knowledge: "The Physical Science Basis," "Impacts, Adaptation, and Vulnerability," and "Mitigation of Climate Change." It clearly summarizes the causes and consequences of climate change. In addition, the "Frequently Asked Questions (FAQs) for The Physical Science Basis" provides clear explanations, with illustrations, of many topics (for example, "What is the Relationship between Climate Change and Weather?" and "How are Temperatures on Earth Changing?") http://www.ipcc.ch.

Dire Predictions: Understanding Global Warming by leading climate scientists Michael E. Mann and Lee R. Kump (New York: Dorling Kindersley, 2008). This book is an illustrated guide to the findings of the Intergovernmental Panel on Climate Change (IPCC). It's a wonderful book with many helpful illustrations that explain the science behind climate change.

The Forgiving Air: Understanding Environmental Change by Richard C. Somerville (Second Edition: American Meteorological Society, 2008). This is a fascinating and understandable book about climate science based on a series of lectures to K12 teachers, by one of the world's top climate scientists.

SALLY RIDE, best known for being the first American woman in space, is Emerita Professor of Physics at the University of California, San Diego. Dr. Ride has B.S, M.S, and Ph.D. degrees in Physics, all from Stanford University. During eight years as a NASA astronaut she flew on two space shuttle missions, served on the President's Commission investigating the space shuttle *Challenger* accident, and headed NASA's long-range planning after the accident. Her flights into space gave her a special perspective on our planet, and while at NASA she championed NASA's "Mission to Planet Earth." Since leaving NASA, Dr. Ride has committed herself to improving science education. She is currently President and CEO of Sally Ride Science, a K12 science education company that creates programs and publications to support students' natural interest in science, and places a special emphasis on encouraging girls. At Sally Ride Science, Dr. Ride initiated the development of a series of science books for the classroom (including a set on "Our Changing Climate") and professional development for educators to help them bring the science behind climate change to the classroom. Dr. Ride has received numerous honors and awards, and has co-authored seven childrens' science books, including *The Third Planet* (co-authored with Tam O'Shaughnessy), which won the American Institute of Physics Children's Science Writing Award.

TAM O'SHAUGHNESSY is Professor Emerita of Education at San Diego State University. Dr. O'Shaughnessy studied biology in college, earning B.S. and M.S. degrees from Georgia State University. While teaching college biology, she became interested in how kids learn and went on to earn a Ph.D. in school psychology from the University of California, Riverside. A former science teacher and award-winning children's science writer, Dr. O'Shaughnessy is currently the COO and Executive Vice President of Sally Ride Science, responsible for all publications and professional development. She oversees the development of Sally Ride Science's classroom books, teacher guides, and educator institutes. In addition, Dr. O'Shaughnessy is the author of ten science books for children, including *Our Changing Climate: Ecosystems* and *The Third Planet* (co-authored with Sally Ride), which won the American Institute of Physics Children's Science Writing Award.

PHOTO CREDITS

INDEX